To Gideon Howard Wolfe
on his first birthday
L. M.

To Jennifer Robin, my first and best playmate
J. M.

First published 2001 by Walker Books Ltd
87 Vauxhall Walk, London SE11 5HJ

2 4 6 8 10 9 7 5 3 1

Text © 2001 Lilian Moore
Illustrations © 2001 Jill McElmurry

The following poems originally appeared in *Humpty Dumpty's Magazine*:
"Snowsuit", "Alone", "Here It Comes", "New Snow", "Ooh!", "Waiting", "Feet",
"Twos", "Finger Paints", "Sand", "Which?", "Scary" and "Growing"

This book has been typeset in Truesdell
The illustrations were done in gouache

Printed in Belgium

British Library Cataloguing in Publication Data:
a catalogue record for this book is
available from the British Library

ISBN 0-7445-7384-X

I'm Small
and other verses

written by **Lilian Moore**

illustrated by **Jill McElmurry**

WALKER BOOKS
AND SUBSIDIARIES
LONDON • BOSTON • SYDNEY

I'm Small

The wind is
    shaking every tree.
The wind is strong
But trees are tall.

The wind is
    pounding every wall.
But walls are strong
And they won't fall.

I think
    I'll hold on
    tight today.
I'm small.

Snowsuit

I'm zipped
    up to my chin.
I like my zipped-up skin.
I like the way it keeps me
    IN.

Alone

I like
　　the way
my fingers feel
　　inside my mitten

Only –

Sometimes
　　I wonder
if my thumb
　　doesn't get quite

Lonely.

Here It Comes

I've a tickly prickly feeling
in the middle of my
nose.

It's a prickly tickly feeling that
goes and comes and
goes.

Now all of me is waiting
and my nose is waiting
too.

We're waiting for a sneeze
to come
and here it comes —

KERCHOO!

Big Snow

Snow says "Hush!"
    to the city,
"Hush your clang
    and din!"
Wraps the streets
    in quiet
And tucks the city in.

New Snow

The new new snow
is sparkling
in the sun.

Wherever I go
in the new new snow
I am
the
very
first one!

I Like Peanut Butter

I like peanut butter
thick
thick
thick.

If it makes my mouth
feel
sticky
stick
stick,

I go for the plum jam
quick
quick
quick.

Ooh!

Ooh!
My arm fell asleep,
And it's strange as can be.
For my arm doesn't feel
Like part of me.

Ooh!
Now that it's waking
How funny it is!
Like ginger ale
That starts to fizz.

Waiting

How long is
"a little while, dear"?
How many days to
"soon"?

Why does the morning
     take so long
To get to
     "this afternoon"?

Feet

Feet
    that wear shoes
Can walk
    and have fun.

Feet
    that wear trainers
Want only
    to run.

Twos

What comes in twos?

Old boots

And new shoes

And gloves to wear going to town

And you and your friend

One on each end

Of a seesaw that goes up and down.

Umbrellas

So many umbrellas
walking,
this grey day.

So many umbrellas
going
every which
way.

Don't worry!
You can find *me*
in a hurry.

My umbrella's
the one
that's
yellow –
like the sun.

Finger Paints

Finger paints are
   cool as mud,
Mud that's red or blue.
They squish and squash
And slide most any
Way I want them to.

I can squeeze a bump of green
Or swish it up and down
Or make it stop
   right on top
Of a humpy hill of brown.

If someone says,
"Do tell us, dear,
What *does* your picture say?"
I swoosh the picture all around
And make it go away!

Sand

Sand pours,
    Sand trickles,
Sand spills,
    Sand tickles.

Sand is cool and wet,
    Sand is warm and dry,
Sand is a castle,
    Sand is a pie.

Most any day
I'd rather play
With sand.

Grey

Blue is sky

Green is grass

Grey is shadow

Where I pass.

Which?

Brick on brick
    I build my tower.
One more,
One more,
    Now it's done.

Will it stand or
    will it crash?
And which,
    oh which,
Would be more fun?

Scary

The mask I'll wear
  on Hallowe'en
Is the scariest one
  you've ever seen.

My face will scare
  most everyone –
But what if my *mother*
  starts to run?

I'll take off my mask
  so she can see
It's only fun. It's
  really ME!

Growing

I'm taller today
  but nobody knows.
I looked in the mirror
  way up on my toes.
For the very first time
  I saw
  my
  NOSE!